✠

This book is dedicated to
Otto Schmieder
with whom I have swapped many a yarn.

✠

Preface

A funny thing happened to our family on the way to church last Sunday. Grandfather told us he almost became a preacher. "It was a hot July on our farm," he recalled. "I was then aged 17 and bored. Studying the stars one night, I told my father I could see the initials 'PC' up there, and I felt they meant 'Preach Christ,' hence I would immediately go forth on my new mission. But father wasn't taken in. 'Wait a few years,' said he wryly. 'Right now, those starry initials you see mean 'plow corn.' "

All right. Grandfather himself went on to become an outstanding Christian farmer, which is better than immature "preachin" would have been. He also developed a fine, gentle sense of humor. The merely pious person can be pitifully stern. But clean, wholesome humor is an exercise of the mind; it is a balancing factor which assures mental and emotional maturity in the individual, and happiness for all concerned.

As with the two preceding books in this series (*Steeple Stories,* and *More Steeple Stories*) that's the premise for this new volume of church-related humor. God bless all who helped me collect it. (*He* obviously has a sense of humor, for man has one, and He made us in His image, didn't He?)

Contents

1.
Clerical Confusion

One morning in service a preacher said, "Our con-
gregation has ten thieves in it, counting Oscar Smith."

After service Oscar naturally jumped him about
that. So next Sunday the preacher told his flock,
"Last week I said we had ten thieves counting Oscar
Smith. Now I apologize to Oscar. What I meant to
say was, we have nine thieves not counting Oscar
Smith."

✛

In Sioux Falls, South Dakota, a pastor was straining
to baptize a baby boy, who celebrated the occasion
by crying loudly. Finally the job was done, and the
good preacher, hoping to assuage the young parents'
embarrassment, said benignly to the congregation,
"What a sweet baby! Baptising him is a pleasure, because it was such a *very* short time ago that I married this couple."

✛

A legal technicality came up in the church business
operation, so Pastor James Murphy called on Elder
Forrest Barton, an attorney. Mr. Barton listened at-
tentively then began, "Well, pastor, if you want my
honest opinion . . ."

"No, no," the distraught preacher interrupted without thinking. "What we need is your professional advice."

The good rabbi trudged home after service, looking blue and despondent. "What was your sermon subject, that took so much starch out of you?" his wife asked.

"Ah, Rachel," said he, "I tried to tell them that it was the duty of the rich to help the poor."

"And did you convince them?" she pursued.

"I guess it was about fifty-fifty. I convinced the poor."

✠

A traffic cop flagged down the Rev. Dr. Woolgatherer, got his name, then snarled, "Oh, so you are a preacher, hey? Now don't go telling me you didn't see that stop sign."

Said the minister, "Oh, to be sure I saw the sign, officer. The point is — I didn't see *you.*"

✠

Every preacher develops a list of chronic pest callers and has to cope with them. One arrived in the outer office at First Presbyterian Church in Phoenix and asked to see Dr. George Hall.

"I do have a slipped disc in my backbone and it is paining me some," George murmured to his secretary, salving his conscience. "So go tell the man that I have an injured back and can't see him this month."

His good secretary duly reported that fact to the caller. But she popped right back into the pastor's study, saying, "He insists on seeing you. He said he didn't come to wrestle with you, but to talk with you."

Another minister and a friend were walking along the sidewalk. The minister stepped on a banana peel, with inevitable results. Next moment he said to his friend, "It's odd how long forgotten words now spring to mind."

✠

Big-city preachers are to be pitied. One of them, long a resident of New York City, came out to Arizona for a vacation. On his very first night at the desert resort hotel, he walked out under the moonless sky with his wife, looked up at the thousands of brightly twinkling stars and exclaimed — "Look, darling, heaven is just like a planetarium!"

✠

The Sunday-school superintendent prevailed on his pastor, the Rev. Aaron Powers, to take the role of Santa Claus.

Well and good. Things went fine. The children were delighted as he ho-ho-hoed in, chuckling and rumbling and handing out toys. It was all so perfect. Finally, he was ready to depart. "See you next Christmas, children," he called. "Ready, Prancer and Dancer, Comet and Vixen?" He made it sound good. The kids waited for the sound of sleigh bells, and heard them sure enough. Perfect showmanship.

But five minutes later poor Santa poked a meek head back in the doorway and beckoned to the superintendent. "Please," he whispered, "would you have everybody look around for my car keys?"

The Rev. Jogalot Jones, who is something of an exercise fanatic, was trotting up a residential street one dawn. Himself a Baptist, he came along in front of the home of a prominent Catholic. Out bounded the yard dog, and it latched firmly onto Dr. Jones' running shorts, growling gently. The good Catholic saw it all and came running to the pastor's aid.

Said Dr. Jones firmly, "Tell your mutt to stop being so ecumenical."

✠

One minister wanted to introduce some new hymn books to his congregation, so he asked his associate minister to notify the group at the end of the sermon. But the associate had a project of his own, an announcement concerning the baptism of babies that day, so at the end of the service he announced, "All those who have children for baptism, please send in their names at once."

The senior minister, preoccupied or distracted, missed that announcement, but assumed that it was the one he ordered about the hymn books. So to clinch it now, he stepped forward and added:

"For the benefit of those who haven't any, please know that they may be obtained from me at any time. The good ones with red backs are $2 each, but the ordinary little ones can be had for only 25 cents each."

✠

A very staid and dignified preacher from Boston came to an Arizona dude ranch for a vacation.

"We've got just the horse for you to ride, parson," said the head wrangler. "He has been trained different from most horses. He don't know 'Giddap' and

'Whoa.' Because we saved him for church folk, we trained him to listen to other commands. If you say, 'Praise the Lord,' he will take off like a streak of lightning. But if you want him to stop, just say 'Amen.'"

Well and good; the minister was pleased. He mounted, said "Praise the Lord," and the horse leaped forward, fast. It was grand, zestful riding. The horse was going at a rapid pace.

But this ranch area was right on top of the famous Tonto Rim. And just yonder a quarter mile was the Rim itself — a sheer drop-off of 2,000 feet straight down. And lo! the preacher discovered that his horse was plunging right toward that Rim! His very life was in danger.

The poor man panicked so that he couldn't think of the word to make the horse stop. But finally he did remember it, and shouted "AMEN!"

Scree-e-e-e-ech! The horse responded; dug his hoofs in, skidded right to the very edge of the Rim where his head hung over.

But the good preacher exhaled, looked up to heaven, put a hand on his brow and said, "Oh, praise the Lord."

✟

It was a bitterly cold day, but the good rural Baptist folk were going to have their Sunday afternoon baptizing regardless. So they cut a hole in the ice, the preacher stepped in up to his waist, and held out a hand for the first sinner, a very husky young woman.

As he dipped her under the water, she slipped out

11

of his icy hands, the current caught her, and she disappeared downstream under the heavy coat of ice.

He stood up, nonplussed, stared a moment, then said to the crowd on the river bank, "Brothers and sisters, hand me down another one. The previous one has just departed."

✠

The rural Kansas parson had been back East on business. When he returned a parishioner met him at the bus station.

"I'm glad to be home," said the parson. "How are things out our way, Hiram?"

"Sad, sir. A cyclone come and wiped my house off the earth."

"Dear, dear," cried the parson. "Well, I am not really surprised, Hiram. You remember that I warned you about the way you had been living. Punishment for sin is inevitable, God will not be mocked. Disasters never come without due cause."

"It also destroyed *your* house, sir," said Hiram.

"IT DID?" The pastor was horrified. "Ah me, the ways of the Lord are past human understanding."

✠

One minister made a very critical error. He preached on "A Fool and His Money Are Soon Parted," just before they passed the collection plate.

✠

"We have tried," said the next pastor, after poor Dr. Thredbaire was gone. "We have tried to raise money for our church without success. We have made an honest effort. Now we are going to hold a bazaar."

Another absent-minded preacher was in the barber chair wrapped in sheet and towel getting a shave. In rushed a parishioner who shouted "Hey, Mr. Johnson, your house is on fire!"

The lathered preacher leaped up, rushed from the shop with sheet trailing, dashed on down the street two blocks, then skidded to a halt.

"What am I running for?" he asked himself. "My name isn't Johnson."

✠

Hard put to know what to say when infants are presented proudly for admiration, most pastors just hedge by exclaiming, "My, my, that *is* a baby, isn't it!"

Then there was this unconventional young minister, who was going to improve on that old tested technique. Up came a young mother holding her little pink baby with mouth open wide.

"What a sweet baby!" the minister cooed. But was it boy or girl? He, too, had to hedge suddenly. "Er — just how old is the — er — the tot?"

"Barely seven weeks, sir," the mother cooed back.

"Well, well," said the flustered young preacher now, "Er — your youngest, I suppose?"

✠

Father Aloysius Hogarty, a good priest, and Moses Plotkin, a beloved rabbi, decided to hire an automobile in Denver and drive out to isolated Rocky Mountain communities to call on members of their respective faiths.

The two friends enjoyed the trip out immensely, and felt that they did a lot of good when they met their people. But on the way home, with Father Aloysius driving, a rainstorm struck them at the top of a steep hill nearly a mile long. Their car started downward.

Presently it began to skid. Plainly it was in danger of dropping off the cliff.

In his terror Father Aloysius instinctively crossed himself.

"Keep your hands on the wheel!" cried his friend the rabbi. "You aren't doing anything for me there!"

✛

Another good priest was going to a backwoods church. At the last bus stop, he had to hire a local yokel to drive him further in an old mule-drawn wagon. Now the yokel saw his chance.

"Father," said he, "they don't know me over there where we are going, so just for fun would you swap clothes with me and see what happens?"

The good-natured priest decided to humor the man, but with this warning: "Do not try to give your ideas of our Catholic doctrine."

Grinning, the man promised, and soon he had on the clerical vestments, while the priest was dressed in a ragged shirt and dirty overalls, driving the mules.

Right after arrival in the village, some man asked the "priest" a very deep question in theology. But the masquerading yokel handled it in fine manner.

"Oh, dear, is *that* the hardest question you could ask me?" he demanded. "Why, even my poor ignorant driver could answer that. Driver, tell these men a thing or two about our faith!"

2.

Congregational Comments

The preacher was taken aback when he overheard this quick bit of talk between two ladies in the church hallway: "Listen carefully, Sue, because I can only tell this once. I promised not to repeat it."

✠

The distinguished Methodist preacher in Hollywood, Dr. Charles S. Kendall, conducts four identical services every Easter Sunday. One Easter in the middle of the third service, two well-dressed ladies quietly got up and walked out. At the door the head usher asked them if one was ill. "Oh no," said they, airily, "this is where we came in."

✠

A postal clerk took the man's package, shook it, squeezed it and asked, "Is anything in here breakable?"

Replied the man, "Yes, The Ten Commandments. It's a Bible."

✠

My family gives me a bad time occasionally. Told my wife I couldn't go to church one Sunday because I was suffering from a severe case of voluntary inertia.

"I'll bet you aren't," that smart cookie answered. "I'll bet you're just lazy."

A missionary in a dark, cannibal jungle saw a man studying him critically, and asked, "Why are you looking at me like that?"

Replied the native, "I am the village food inspector."

✠

For almost 30 years, Dr. Clarence G. Salsbury served at Ganado, Arizona, bringing the Gospel to Navajo and Hopi Indians, and to a few whites as well. During his first years there, Dr. Salsbury was busily constructing hospital and school buildings, and because they quickly learned to love and respect the Big White Doctor, most of the Indians were glad to furnish the labor. But one husky red man, Bull Snakesausage, was a born freeloader. Whenever Dr. Salsbury sent word to Bull that manpower was needed, Bull sent back a message: "Me can't come, me too busy." Then he would drop off to sleep again.

That state of affairs existed for more than a year, until one day, a runner came in near panic to Dr. Salsbury. "Doctor, Doctor, come quick! Bill Snakesausage is dying. A man has rammed a pitchfork into his belly!"

That was, of course, an emergency call indeed, but Dr. Salsbury remained calm. "Go back and tell my friend Snakesausage," said the doctor, "that I said, 'Me can't come, me too busy.'"

Horrified, the runner sped back with the message.

Dr. Salsbury waited just 60 seconds — time enough for the runner to get out of sight. Then he took off, drove to poor Bull's nearby hogan, attended the man, and saved his life. A month later Bull Snake-sausage was as good as new again.

Next week Dr. Salsbury sent his bill: "Tell friend Snakesausage we start work tomorrow morning on a new wing for the hospital."

Bull was there before dawn, a volunteer laborer who worked hardest of all, through that summer and ever after whenever needed.

✠

Another time Dr. Salsbury heard about an Indian who had five wives, so he rode over to remonstrate with him.

"You are violating a law of God and a law of the United States," said the good missionary. "So you just go in your hogan and tell four of those women they can no longer live here or consider you their husband."

The placid Indian gave a few moments of silent thought to the matter, then said, "Me wait here. You tell 'em."

✠

This story is told:

One autumn, the Notre Dame football machine was traveling to Dallas to play Southern Methodist University. A reporter met them at the airport and said, "Is it true that you carry a chaplain along to pray for the Notre Dame team?"

"Certainly," the coach nodded.

"Could I interview him?"

"Of course. Which one do you want, our offensive or defensive chaplain?"

17

Many hymns, like many parables, need interpretation, especially for youth. I had to go to college before I learned what "sheaves" were, although for years I had sung about bringing them in.

✠

The young minister was high; the Lord had blessed his home with a baby boy and his wife was in good health. So he telegraphed his rather worldly mother this thrifty message: "Isaiah 9:6."

Mom got the message. She telephoned her husband at his office and said: "A telegram came. George and Martha evidently have had a boy who weighs nine pounds and six ounces, and they have named him Isaiah."

✠

Kindly old Dr. Saddlie Thredbaire was being very patient with peppery Mrs. Weems of his parish. It was October, and he was explaining that the big baseball teams would soon be starting their campaigns to decide who was world champion.

"My goodness," she exclaimed, "I thought they settled that last *October!"*

✠

A man called the Rev. Dr. Crane. Now he was always available to parishioners, some of whom wanted their conferences with him kept secret. But the new church secretary purred, "May I ask who is calling him, please?"

"Sure," our man replied. "*I* am the person who is calling Dr. Crane."

The call went right through.

Have you heard about the preacher who called another one on the long distance telephone? It was a parson-to-parson call.

✠

Rev. James Regester, pastor of First Presbyterian Church in Thompsonville, Connecticut, had a practice of leaving his pulpit for ten minutes during the morning service. While one of the elders took over, he ducked out to tell a Bible story to a class of children in Sunday school.

A newcomer didn't understand. One day he said to the minister, "Rev. Jim, you are the first preacher I ever saw who took a coffee break during service."

✠

The evangelist was preaching, and in the middle of it a layman jumped up and took the floor. "Brethren!" he shouted. "I have been a miserable, contemptible sinner for years, and never knew it before tonight!" A deacon in the nearby aisle shushed him. "Sit down, Brother. The rest of us knew it all the time."

✠

The Right Reverend and Very Distinguished Dr. Lexicon Glossology, a professor from Doldrum Theological and Ideological Seminary, was being interviewed on the subject of "Presumptuous Polysyllabification." Things went along fine for twenty of the allotted thirty minutes on the air, but then the interviewer stopped the show.

"Thank you very much, Dr. Glossology. We won't have time for another question, and most certainly we wouldn't have time for another answer."

"*Have you got the price of a meal, mister?*" a pan-handler asked poor old Dr. Thredbaire.

"*No,*" replied he. "*But don't worry; I'll manage somehow.*"

✠

A prominent Frenchman was visiting the U.S.A. and one of our reporters asked him what he thought of President de Gaulle.

"I am an atheist," replied the man. "There is no de Gaulle."

✠

When Marie Walling took temporary leave of her job as Church Editor for *The Arizona Republic*, the publisher appointed its Farm Editor, Bob Thomas, to fill in for Marie.

"Great!" exclaimed Bob. "Now I have a new title. I am Editor of Heaven and Earth!"

✠

A pastor was at the circus, testing the performers' faith. "I have faith in *you* to do your dangerous work," said he. "You must have faith in God."

The tightrope walker asked, from high up in the tent, "Do you have faith in me to walk this rope?"

"Yes," said the preacher.

"Do you think I can push this wheelbarrow as I walk across the tent on this high rope?"

"Yes, even that. I believe in you."

"The climb up here, sir, and ride across in the wheelbarrow."

Throughout the summer, especially in the southwestern states, ranch folks often meet outdoors for worship services. Frequently they select some beautiful tree that stands apart, perhaps on a hill, and assemble in its shade. Few women attend; more often it is a dozen or so sunburned men who ride up, dismount and sit on the ground there. There may be no organized service at all, and may be little talk for a while. Presently some old cowpoke who might well pose as a villain in a novel, will bow his head and say, "Good Lord, it's moughty fine just to be settin' here with You. Talk to us now, please Sir."

On one such occasion about 250 men gathered with more than normal concern showing in their faces. All looked to one gray-haired leader to do the talking, so after a proper interval of quiet he removed his hat, raised up on his knees, looked to the sky and said, "Lord A'mighty, it ain't rained around here in nigh onto seven months. Our grass is dried up, our cattle is dying, things look bad. Please, Sir, figure out some way to get some rain sent down here. Amen."

The sky at that moment was completely cloudless as it had been for many a long, weary week. Two hours later rain began.

It came in such torrents, and lasted so many days, that the men all met back there again the next Sunday under the same tree, dripping wet now. And the same elderly man again spoke for himself and his neighbors: "Good Lord, Sir, it's true that we needed rain, and it's true that we prayed for it. But this here flood, Lord, is getting ridiculous!"

The Rev. Bill Vogel missed his plane, stood there looking at his watch, then angrily drove back to town with it and stopped at the fine jewelry store operated by his parishioner, Otto Schmieder.

"I had faith in this watch," he told Otto, "but it has failed me."

Otto inspected the watch quickly, then said, "Well, pastor, you should know that faith is not enough without good works."

✠

Julian McConley was a highly educated, highly experienced musician who directed a big choir and a big orchestra. One day he was playing golf. Every time he swung a club, the ball went wild. His exasperation mounted by the minute, until finally he asked his caddy, "What am I doing wrong? What's the matter with me?"

Said the astute caddy, "Mister, you just ain't got rhythm."

✠

Mrs. Barker, Director of Music for the big, fashionable downtown church, was also highly trained; she held degrees in Musicology and Musicianship from a half dozen distinguished schools. She not only directed the choir, she conducted the 30-piece church orchestra, and often combined the two groups for a magnificent service. One Wednesday night for rehearsal, she had the orchestra at seven o'clock and the choir — in the next room — at eight.

Some of the choir gathered a little early, and of course overheard the instrumentalists. When eight o'clock came and Mrs. Barker entered the choir room, the First Soprano gushed — "That last little thing the orchestra did was so charming. I loved its wild abandon, its ultra modern theme. Was it your own composition?"

"No," said Mrs. Barker drily. "That was the violin section re-tuning their instruments."

✠

You can't trust that new young minister at our church; he has fouled up established routine most embarrassingly. He doesn't stand at the door to shake hands with worshipers after the service, he hastens out to the curb and shakes hands with the red-faced parents waiting for their children to come out of Sunday school.

✠

Scottish people are noted for their thrift. For example, there was Scotty McInnes who made a serious error in his church near Princes Street, Edinburgh, one Sabbath morn. Instead of his usual penny in the collection plate, he inadvertently dropped in two shillings.

The matter distressed him greatly, of course. He discussed it at length with his sweet wife. He walked the moors, reflecting. He prayed. He brooded. Finally he came to a conclusion, and so for the next 23 Sundays he ignored the collection plate entirely, knowing full well that a shilling represented 12 pence.

His friends thoroughly understood and sympathized, so nought was said. Until, on the 24th Sunday, Scotty still ignored the collection plate.

But he didn't get by with it. The beadle had been keeping tabs. Today he shook the plate forcefully under Scotty's nose again and spoke out — "Your time is up noo, Scotty."

We have a lot of weddings in our church sanctuary. I often take my wife and daughters. They get the same emotional workouts that the movies give them, and it's a whole lot cheaper.

✠

One preacher also was an author. One day he telephoned a big movie studio in Hollywood and offered to sell a scenario entitled "Pilate's Wife." The Hollywood mogul replied, "No sale. We have had too many airplane pictures already."

✠

The good pastor was in his study early one morning, preparing next Sunday's sermon. The telephone rang, he answered and heard a frantic female voice.

"Oh, Rev. Smith, please hurry over to our house! The doctor is coming, but we need you too."

"Now just be calm, madam, if there is an emergency. What is the trouble?"

"When my husband got up a little while ago, he swallowed his tranquilizer, his vitamins, his ulcer capsule, two antihistimines, his anti-fat pill, his anti-depressant, and two spoonfuls of benzadrine. Then, when he lighted his morning cigarette, there was this terrible explosion!"

✠

A handsome young clergyman felt it his duty to reprimand the college girls' Sunday-school class about the way they costumed themselves. "The more experience I have with lipstick," said he, "the more distasteful I find it."

3.
Front Lines

The new Army recruit was given guard duty at 2 a.m. He did his best for a while, but about 4 a.m. he went to sleep. He awakened to find the Officer of the Day standing before him.

Remembering the heavy penalty for being asleep on guard duty, this smart-thinking young man kept his head bowed for another moment, then looked piously upward and reverently said, "A-a-a-a-men!"

✝

The Army chaplain called on George Goofoff, injured and in the hospital. "Mighty sorry you have been shot, George," said the good man, somewhat warily. He suspected only minor wounds.

George groaned. "Yes, chaplain. I got so many bullet holes through me the fellow behind me complained of the draft."

"Don't doubt it at all. In fact, I can see through you myself."

✝

Another chaplain was visiting the warship's sick bay. A young sailor complained about a sore throat.

"Have you tried gargling salt water?" the chaplain suggested.

The boy rasped, "You ask me that, sir, who has been torpedoed four times?"

The raw recruit in the Marines was about to be severely disciplined and his chaplain tried to comfort him. "What did you do, son?" the chaplain asked.

"Sir, I only answered a question," pleaded the boy.

"What question?"

"Well sir, the drill sergeant says to me, 'What do you think I am?' and I told him."

✠

At an advanced Marine base in Vietnam a good Catholic chaplain was put in charge of Protestant services. But the Protestant hymns were strange to him. He couldn't think how to start one, although the reverent Marines kept very quiet.

Finally a big Texas sergeant spoke up, "That's all right, Chaplain. We'll take care of the singing, sir. You just give us the dickens."

✠

It seems that the chaplain of the Air Force Base was called away on urgent business. But before leaving he asked a sergeant to read the Episcopalian prayer service in his absence.

The sergeant struggled with it, doing well at first. He read the Call to Worship, the Invocation, led the men through the Confession of Sins, then read the Absolution of Sins for them. As he finished, he noticed in the rubrics (the small italics which describe the performance of the service) that this was to be done only by an ordained minister; no mere sergeant could read them the Absolution of Sins.

But this sergeant was resourceful, and his service training came to the fore. He looked up and intoned, "As you were, men!"

A Navy chaplain was on a warship in the far Pacific. One of his favorite seamen, Butch Boswell, was due for discharge the next day. The chaplain was a very patriotic man, and he was trying to argue Butch into re-enlistment.

"Honestly now, son, you don't really want to leave the Navy and waste four years of valuable experience and training, do you?"

"Yes, sir, chaplain, I do," Butch replied. "You see, sir, I also have 22 years of very valuable experience and training as a civilian which I don't want to waste."

✛

Up near the dangerous front somewhere in Vietnam one of our Army chaplains was conducting worship services. Artillery explosions were heard nearby, right in the middle of the chaplain's prayer. He paused in mid-sentence and spoke louder. "Is that outgoing or incoming?"

Together the reverent soldiers answered, "Outgoing, sir."

The chaplain reverently resumed his prayer right in the middle of that sentence where he had stopped.

✛

A young recruit had been in boot camp for a month. The training instructor had been zealous, as always. The boy was a good Catholic, and when the chaplain announced that confessions would be heard next morning, the lad asked permission to go.

"All right, son," the instructor agreed. "But just tell me this — in the past four weeks, just when have I given you time enough to do anything wrong?"

During wartime the usual crowd thronged the railroad station. A glamor girl in a bridal veil was waving to her soldier on the rear platform of an outgoing train. Suddenly her face showed panic. She ran down the track, shouting, "Darling, sweetheart, I forgot to ask you. *What is our last name?*"

✞

The handsome young ex-Marine came home with a beautiful young wife that he had married in Tokyo. The home town preacher made it his business to interview the "foreign" bride and bid her welcome.

"How are you and Henry getting along?" he asked, smiling. "No family quarrels yet, I hope?"

"No clarl," she enchanted him with her version of English, her bright smile. "He mad me, he shout Eengleesh. Me mad heem, me shout Lapanees. Nobody unnerstan, nobody care. Much love."

✞

Charles de Gaulle, the great French leader, was often accused of nursing a superiority complex; people said he took credit for everything good in France. Allegedly, an American diplomat was visiting him one April, when the flowers of Paris were in full magnificent bloom, the sun was beaming, the air was zestful and cool. As the two men strolled along, the American said, "My, my, General, what a glorious day!"

Intoned the General, "Thank you."

4.
Homespun Homilies

If you must start a whispering campaign in church, start by whispering a prayer.

✛

Too many well-meaning people wait for the hearse to bring them to church.

✛

"There must be something in reincarnation after all," grumbled Deacon Dunlap, boss of a big factory. "If you doubt it, just visit my place sometime and watch the help come back to life at quitting time."

✛

"We must all expect change, for it is inevitable," gently explained the Rev. Roy Shepler to his flock. "But we can all decide whether it is to be by consent or coercion."

✛

"If you do somebody a favor, try not to remember it," the lady Sunday-school teacher told her class. "If somebody does you a favor, try not to forget it."

✛

"My wife talks to herself very often," admits kindly old Rev. Dr. McIntyre, who is semiretired from our church, "but she doesn't know it. She thinks I am listening."

✝

"It is hard to feel that life on Mars is possible," rumbled the somewhat fedup pastor to his congregation one day, *"when so often it seems impossible here on earth."*

✝

"No, sir, young man," the fine old pastor counseled an eager high school junior who wanted to be a dropout. "It is *not* always a bright idea to strike out for yourself — for instance, in baseball."

✝

"The route of all evil," says good Rev. Saddlie Thredbaire, "is Easy Street."

✝

"The future is changing," rumbled wise old Rev. Peabody with a twinkle in his eye. "It now gets here a lot quicker than it used to."

✝

Faith — we are told — is that quality which enables you to eat blackberry jam at a church picnic without looking closely to see if the seeds move.

✝

One thing about Noah — he didn't miss the boat.

In these times of high fiduciary finagling everywhere, it is interesting to note that Noah was the greatest financier who ever lived. He was able to float a company when the whole world was in liquidation.

✠

This was a very wise old minister. For half a century he had kept prominently on his desk a notebook labeled COMPLAINTS OF MEMBERS. Whenever any member of his church came in to tattle on somebody else's conduct, the fine old pastor would nod and pick up the notebook, saying, "Thank you, I'll just write it down so that I can take it up officially with the church board."

The book and the poised pen worked like magic. Although the opportunity was offered hundreds of times, nothing was ever written in the book. The plaintiffs never quite showed a willingness to go through with it.

✠

"Worship at church is not 'the service,'" warns Pastor Albert Hjerpe. "The service begins when the worshiper leaves the church."

✠

Sir, you need only to mumble a few words in your church to get married — a few words in your sleep to get divorced.

"If you would get on the road to heaven," advises Pastor Jim Mordy, "turn right and keep going straight."

✠

Most appropriate of all songs for the choir to sing just after the morning sermon? "Awake, Ye Sinners!"

✠

Certainly liberalism has its place in all our churches, especially if you demonstrate yours in the collection plate.

✠

Do you want to know why Daniel wasn't devoured in the lions' den? Because most of him was backbone and the rest of him was grit.

✠

Any Sunday-school teacher is a person whose job is to welcome a lot of live wires and see that they are well grounded.

✠

"A gold digger?" mused the parson, asked to define the term. "That's a girl who hates poverty worse than sin."

✠

"Ecumenical" is a good church word that hasn't really caught on very well. But I'm not surprised. It is much too etymological.

32

Pastor P. Con Crunch says: "There are many people who are serenely satisfied with mediocrity. Their lives are records of negativism. They have done nothing bad; worse, they have done nothing good, either."

✛

Preacher Horace Voice says: "A political party gets into debt. It gives a series of $100-a-plate dinners at which a dollar's worth of food is served.

"A church gets into debt. It gives a series of 50-cent dinners at which a dollar's worth of food is served."

✛

Do any of you good steeple people know the difference between a church bell and a politician?

Well, one peals from the steeple, the other steals from the people.

✛

Certainly Americans trust in God, says Pastor Crunch. You can tell that by the way they drive.

✛

"If our baritones were less barren and our tenors more tenable," says our choir director, "we'd have less heterogeneous harmony and more mellifluous melody."

✛

Many of our church leaders keep telling us that we are at the end of one great era or epoch, and at the beginning of another. As an old horse-and-buggy Texan, I'm not sure what they mean, even though I suspect they may be right.

✠

In trying times, the temptation is to stop trying.

✠

The new man in our church is a fine Christian scholar and gentleman. His views of religion, football, politics, fishing, women, taxes and Communism coincide exactly with mine.

✠

This wonderful old story, heard many times, is said to have originated when Henry Thoreau, the great naturalist, was dying. A pious aunt asked him, "Henry, have you made your peace with God?"

Said Henry, "I didn't know that we had ever quarrelled."

✠

Generally speaking, preachers are.

✠

Charlie Kendall, a Methodist minister in Hollywood, and I spent two pleasant hours recently listing the differences between Methodists and Presbyterians. We came up with a couple of hot ones: (1) Methodists eat more, because there are more of them. (2) Presbyterians sleep more, because our ministers are quieter.

5.
Impenitent Pilgrims

"All the world is in the same boat nowadays," rumbled Mr. Bimson the banker. "That means we haven't progressed much since the time of Noah."

✝

Somebody put a bunch of empty whiskey bottles into the garbage can owned by teetotaler Horatio Bartle. "I was horrified," said he at church. "Just imagine my embarrassment. I got them out of there in a hurry, because I didn't want the garbage men to think I drink."

"Natch," a friend agreed. "But what did you do with them?"

"Well, as you know, Reverend Green lives next door, so I put the bottles in his can. Everybody knows he doesn't drink."

✝

Attorney Patrick W. O'Reilly, a good Christian, was examining a witness in court. He had begun to suspect the man of perjury, so he asked very emphatically, "Do you understand the nature of an oath?"

"'Course I do," the man replied.

"And do you also realize that the Bible commands you not to bear false witness against your neighbor?"

"Sure, I know that too. I ain't bearing false witness *against* him, I'm bearing it for him."

The very blonde and beautiful Miss Angela Auerglas joined the church choir, a newcomer who caught everybody's eye. After service that Sunday, the young minister's wife coyly asked him, "You wouldn't trade me in for that Angela Auerglas, would you Herbert?"

Smirking just a trifle, Herbert replied, "No, I wouldn't think of trading you in for her. I would keep you as a spare."

✠

The good minister called at the home of Fred Frugal when he learned that Fred was seriously ill in the hospital; he wanted to comfort the wife and see if he might call on Fred himself.

"Oh, Fred's improving," said the wife airily, "but he is still in the expensive-care department."

✠

In Shaugh Prior, England, the Rev. John Byrnell was helping his wife do the supper dishes. "This isn't a man's job," said the pastor, in mild masculine protest.

"Oh, yes it is," retorted Mrs. Byrnell. "In II Kings 21:13 it says '. . . and I will wipe Jerusalem as a man wipeth a dish, wiping it and turning it upside down.'"

Rev. Byrnell was so surprised that he dropped the plate.

✠

Baseball coaches may understand baseball, but do not necessarily understand choral music. Coach Winkles had a pretty wife who joined the church choir.

"How you doin', sugar?" he asked her later.

"All right, I guess," said she, modestly. "I sing second soprano."

Coach looked grim. "Second! That ain't good enough. Tell you what, I'll send that choir director a couple of complimentary tickets to our next game. Then maybe he'll make you *first* soprano!"

✠

America has thousands of new church buildings, most of which are beautiful. But some are unconventional, and the people complain. "The life of a church architect," declared one of them, "is a constant battle with laymen who think the only way to heaven is through a Gothic arch."

✠

"By the time the meek inherit the earth," growled Old Man Gotrocks, "the taxes will be so high they can't keep it."

✠

A former pastor came back to town twenty years later and visited a once impecunious friend. "My, my, Henry," said the preacher, "I hear that you have struck it rich, and I am so glad to see that great wealth has not changed you."

"Oh, but it has, pastor," declared the millionaire. "When you were here, people called me impolite; now they call me 'eccentric.' And where I used to be rude, I am now 'delightfully witty.'"

A certain man had spent all his life making money. Wealthy now, he decided to join a church. Because of his importance they promptly made him an elder. Then to his horror, one Sunday morning the minister called on him to lead in prayer.

Well, he rose to the occasion, we could say. Though thoroughly distraught, the rich man closed his eyes and began: "Now I lay me down to sleep. . . ."

✠

Sin is sin, and never ye forget it. In Scotland a young pastor lived five miles up river from his church, and one Sunday the river was frozen over and the roads were blocked by snow. The brave young man would not be denied; he simply skated down river to his church.

But the church elders promptly accused him of breaking the Sabbath. He explained it was the only way he could get to his pulpit.

"Niver mind that," the spokesman scowled. "Just ye answer the main question: did ye, or did ye not enjoy the skatin'?"

✠

At laymen's meetings there are too many speakers who need no introductions. What they need are conclusions.

✠

The trouble with too many church socials is that they open at 7:30 sharp and close at 10:30 dull.

✠

How wonderful is American life! Up in Connecticut in a small town, the bell in the tall Baptist Church tower rings out loudly at a fairly early hour each Sunday morning. But not a soul can be seen responding, nobody approaches the church at all. An hour later it rings again, and immediately the people stream out of their homes going toward the sanctuary.

You see, a block or two away is a Catholic Church, but it has no tower bell. That first tolling by the Baptist bell, then, is to call the Catholic faithful to their church for mass.

Hurray for the American people!

✠

Scotty McDonald fell into the lake, and Irishman Patrick O'Reilly pulled him out.

"You should give your friend Patrick a dollar for saving your life," suggested Scotty's minister very generously.

Scotty considered the matter at length, and with great solemnity finally asked, "Could I make it fifty cents, pastor? I was half dead when he pulled me out."

✠

Dr. Straightlace was walking up the street of his town, and met a parishioner. "George," he began severely, "your good wife tells me that your conduct has been reprehensible. Now, why don't you take a lesson from me? I can go to the shopping center and back home again without getting inebriated."

"Ah, yes, Your Reverence," poor George agreed, "maybe you can, sir. But you see, sir, you are not as popular as I am."

✠

It seems that the prominent church member had

passed on without apparent cause, and the preacher demanded an investigation and got it. Soon, however, the coroner's jury reported to him: "The man died from an act of God under very auspicious circumstances."

✠

His Reverence, the very citified Dr. Pompous, had been called to the new park to dedicate a statue near a giant tree. "Oh great oak," he chanted, eyes uplifted, "if you could speak down through the centuries, what would you say to the people gathered here?"

An honest cynic stage-whispered, "First thing, it would say, 'Pardon me, sir, but I happen to be an elm.'"

✠

The parson, calling on farm folk, came onto a farmer having a hassle with a mule. "Why don't you get rid of that stubborn animal?" he asked.

The farmer relaxed a bit, glaring at the mule, then said, "Parson, if I traded him off he would regard that as a personal victory. For two years he has been trying to get rid of *me!*"

✠

Shiftless Sam the village loafer encountered the preacher, who sought to question him. "Sam, have you stolen any chickens this week?"

"No suh, not nary a chicken." Sam stood humbly, hat in hand.

"Any turkeys?"

"No, suh, not a single turkey, suh."

"All right, have you stolen any pigs?"

"Pahson, how kin you ask! I never steals any pigs."

"Very well," the good man started off. *"Just see to it that you stay in the paths of righteousness."*

Sam mopped his brow and trudged on home, where he reported his narrow escape to his wife Ellie. "I sho was lucky," said he. "If he had asked me about ducks, I would have been lost."

✠

Ike and Abe, two hulking country citizens, never did get along well, and the parson despaired of ending their feud. But the time came when Ike was critically ill, and the pastor called.

"Ike," said the kindly man, "I want you now to forgive Abe and end that long enmity before you go."

"You sayin' I'm gonna die, rev-rend?"

"It looks as if you might."

Ike considered that, then said, "Well, okay, parson, I forgive him. But if I do get up from here and get my health back, that lyin' scoundrel sure better high-tail it out of this county!"

✠

"Yes," said the preacher, back from a summer trip to Hawaii, "we had great adventure. Our ship leaked and slowed down, and a lone shark followed us for days."

"Heavens!" growled one listener, who no doubt was experienced. "Those loan sharks are everywhere!"

✠

The service was over, and a young father was shaking the hand of the minister at the church door. "In your sermon today, pastor," said the young man, "you spoke of a baby's being a new wave on the ocean of life."

41

"Ah, yes," beamed the minister benevolently.

"Well, sir, don't you think 'a fresh squall' would have been closer to the truth?"

✠

"It is true," intoned the unctuous minister, "that life begins at forty."

One matter of fact lady in the third pew spoke up, perhaps louder than she meant to: "Begins to what?"

✠

A stranger arrived at church late, and dutifully listened to the sermon which went on, and on, and on. Finally he turned to his pew neighbor and whispered, "How long has he been preaching here?"

"Five years," the other man whispered back.

"I'll wait, then," said our boy. "He should be through before long."

✠

A fine old Scottish gardener was taken to Edinburgh to see an exhibition of paintings. His host asked what he thought about one great picture titled "The Fall."

"'Tis not authentic," ruled the gardener. "Eve is tempting Adam with an apple variety that was not known until aboot thirty years ago."

✠

Four philosophical gents were outlining their ideas for world salvation. Said one, "Now if we could just eliminate all profanity, this would be a better world."

Said another, "If we could eliminate all liquor, we would have a better world."

Said a third, "Aye, if we could get rid of those and

all other sinful things, we would have a millennium."

At which point the fourth philosopher growled, "Yes, and then we would have that to put up with!"

✠

At a session of church trustees one little-minded man kept popping off in such a way as to make himself appear silly. Finally the distinguished chairman arose, took charge of the meeting and said, "In the days of Balaam it was considered a miracle when an ass spoke. But times have changed."

✠

The auctioneer was in fine form: "Step up a little closer, ladies and gents. Now tell me, what am I offered for this beautiful marble bust of Charles Dickens?"

Said a man out front, "That's not Dickens, that's Shakespeare."

"It is? Ha, ha, well the joke is sure on me. Just shows what I know about The Bible."

✠

The Rev. Sam Lindamood had heard parishioner Pat O'Reilly tell about a certain big fish at intervals for two weeks, and finally decided it was his duty to remonstrate with Pat. "I have noticed, Mr. O'Reilly, that when you tell about the fish you caught, it varies in size for different listeners. How about that?"

"Oh, parson, I have to be realistic," explained Pat. "I never tell a man more than I think he will believe."

✠

Snuffy Smith was a constant problem to the

preacher. Snuffy was not above gambling, or even occasional bits of thievery. One day the minister found Snuffy dancing in rage and frustration, and asked him what was the matter.

"My wife left the door of the chicken house open and every last chicken got out!"

"Well, now, just calm yourself, Snuffy. You know that chickens always come home to roost."

"But parson, them chickens will go home to roost!"

✙

The good preacher visiting a penitentiary came onto a convict busily at work on canvas bags and tarps. "What are you doing, my man?" asked he. "Sewing?"

"Nah," growled the convict. "Reaping."

✙

Conscience, we are told, is the still small voice which tells us that somebody is looking.

✙

A church-going father and his small son were out duck hunting. Dad kept telling sonny what a good shot he was. Presently a lone duck flew over, and father took careful aim and fired. The duck kept right on flying.

But father was not upset. He turned to the boy and said, "Son, you have just witnessed a miracle. There flies a dead duck."

✙

The studious ten-year-old boy said to his

44

father, "What does the Chaplain of Congress do?"

Replied the realistic dad, "He stands up, takes a look at the Congressmen, then prays for the country."

✛

The old man was a strict Sabbatarian. When his son came back from college and said he had earned money by delivering milk, even on Sundays, the father was upset.

"Well, why not deliver?" the boy demanded. "Cows give milk on Sundays."

"Well," said the old man, "they ought not."

✛

The circuit-riding pastor rode his horse far out back of beyond, and called at a rural home. Only a girl seemed to be there, so he asked to speak to her father.

"Cain't speak to him," she explained. "Pap's in the penitentiary."

"Well then, your mother maybe?"

"Nawp. She's been took to the hosspittle. She was seein' things."

"Ah, sad," the minister shook his head. "But perhaps I could speak with your brother."

"Oh, Sebe. Why brother's away at Harvard University."

The good preacher brightened. "How nice! What is he studying?"

"He ain't studyin' nuthin'," said the girl. "They're studyin' him."

The new organist at the church was seen to scowl and grimace every Sunday during the hymns and anthems. Finally the minister asked him, "Why do you seem so unhappy when you play?"

Snarled the man, "I hate music."

✠

The lady had been bitten by a rabid dog. Her minister, knowing hydrophobia to be a horrifying and incurable disease, called on her and tactfully suggested that she write her last words before the vicious part of the disease struck. She agreed, got pen and paper and began writing while he waited. She wrote, and wrote, and wrote. Finally the preacher inquired about it.

"Rather a long will, isn't it, Sister Jones?"

"Will?" she looked at him with a fiendish glint in her eye. "Who's writing a will? This is a list of the people I intend to bite."

✠

The old church building needed remodeling, and it was going to cost plenty of money, so the preacher got up and made impassioned appeal, looking directly at the richest man in town, Mr. Gottmillion.

At the end of the appeal, Mr. Gottmillion stood up and said, "Pastor I agree that the church needs repairs. I will contribute $1,000."

Just then, plaster fell from the ceiling and struck Mr. Gottmillion on the shoulder. He promptly stood again and said, "Pastor, I will increase my donation to $5,000."

Before he could sit back down, plaster fell on him

again, and again he spoke, "Pastor, on second thought, I will contribute $10,000."

He sat down, and a really big chunk of plaster fell, hitting him this time on the head. He stood once more and said, "Pastor, I will give $20,000!"

This prompted Deacon Jones to shout, "Hit him again, Lord, hit him again!"

✠

"What's the idea of the black band of mourning on your ankle, Paddy?" a friend asked.

Paddy said, "Me mother has passed away."

"But why on your ankle instead of your sleeve?"

"She was me stepmother."

✠

A distinguished minister and psychologist had spent the morning counselling members of his flock, one by one. The last caller was a seedy looking man with a turkey feather sticking out the top of his hat, and with a strip of raw bacon hanging from each ear.

But the minister had long ago schooled himself to show surprise at nothing. Said he, "Now what can I do for you, sir?"

"Doc," said the caller, "I came about my brother. He ain't normal."

✠

The glum-faced fellow was sitting before a well-known minister, who of course was trying to help him. "You say that you have failed in every business you have tried," the good preacher said. "You speak only of failure."

"That's right," the man nodded, eyes downcast.

"Well, now!" the famous minister spoke heartily. "I say to you, sir, that you must get the power of positive thinking. You must forget failure, and think positively, never negatively. You can start right now. Will you do that?"

"Yes, sir," the poor pilgrim nodded, showing a mild spark of life. "I see what you mean. So now I know that positively I am going to fail again."

✠

The big debate between William Jennings Bryan and Clarence Darrow was under way. Both were erudite men. Bryan held out for the literal interpretation of The Bible, Darrow took a somewhat broader view to say the least.

During a recess, a reporter asked Mr. Darrow, "Sir, how does it feel to be debating with a distinguished Bible scholar?"

"I wouldn't know," snapped Darrow. "Ask Bryan."

✠

It was January, and the temperature was near freezing, but the zealous minister was baptizing a newly converted prevaricator before the man could slip backward into sin again. Several deacons were on hand as witnesses.

The man was lowered under the water then lifted up, and the kindly minister asked, "Is it cold?"

"No-o-o!" replied the convert through chattering teeth.

You'd better dunk him again, parson," a deacon urged. "He ain't quit lying yet."

6.
Printer's Panic

Up in Spokane the church bulletin editor got a little careless with some questions and answers, as witness this listing:

"What Makes God Tired?"
Dr. Emerson and Choir.

✠

At the Second Presbyterian Church of Bloomington, Illinois, a few years ago the Sunday bulletin with the Order of Worship always carried the words of "The Apostle's Creed," including that ineptly worded phrase, "He descended into hell." To appease people who misunderstood that phrase, an asterisk was printed beside it, and small-type explanation given below.

But normally also, an asterisk was printed four times in the upper part of the page, as a guide for the ushers.

One Sunday, the printer had goofed. There were no asterisks above, but there was one beside "He descended into hell." And down at the bottom of the page in footnote position beside the matching asterisk were these words: "Ushers will seat latecomers here."

✠

A Minnesota newspaper in reporting a wedding stated that the soprano sang "O Previous Love."

At Needles, California, every August the thermometer soars to 120 degrees F. and more as a matter of daily routine. So one opportunist minister put this sign on his outdoor church bulletin board:
YOU THINK IT'S HOT HERE?

✝

A collect is a special mass. Father J. D. Connally, pastor of Saint Vincent de Paul Church, sent the local newspaper an announcement that there would be no collects during the Lenten services.

Of course, the paper erred. It stated there would be no collections *during Lent!*

✝

A music store in Lewistown, Idaho, reported that a choir leader had ordered the anthem, "The Lord Is Exhausted."

✝

In Seattle, one bulletin reported an afternoon gathering: "The Lady's Ade Will Serve Lemonaid."

✝

A big city paper reported: "Miss McIntyre's insipid singing caused the congregation to burst into applesauce."

✝

Wry sign posted on a university campus: "The end of the world has been postponed until next semester due to a shortage of harps and trumpets."

A printed sign in London said: "Seventy-five per cent of the English clergy read *The Times.*"

Underneath it, some wag had printed: "The other twenty-five per cent buy it."

✠

An eager young man wanted a job as editor on a newspaper. The hard-boiled publisher said, "All right, I'll give you a job if you can show talent. Now what headline would you put on this kind of story: At 3 o'clock in the morning, a young couple got a preacher out of bed, and asked him to marry them."

"That's easy," said the applicant. I'd headline it: 'Parson Ties Knot In Shirttail.'"

✠

A well known bishop arrived in town with a flourish, ready to make a masterful speech at church on Sunday. On Saturday morning a cub reporter interviewed him. The bishop felt expansive, told the young man many of his finest anecdotes and incidents. "But don't print these, son," he admonished. "I plan to use them in my address tomorrow, and I want them to be fresh."

The reporter agreed, and in the afternoon paper his write-up of the interview concluded with this statement: "The bishop told a number of good stories which can not be printed."

✠

Sign posted in a church hallway:
RELIGION WILL DO JUST AS MUCH
FOR YOU AS YOU DO FOR IT.

This face-the-facts notice allegedly was posted in a church in Scotland: "Worshipers in the habit of putting buttons instead of coins in the collection plate, are asked to put in their own buttons, and not those from the pew cushions."

✠

The following amusing and highly interesting news appeared in a church folder in the Northwest: "In the absence of the Reverend .... while on vacation, the assistant minister, Rev. ...., will have charge of all pastoral cuties."

✠

This make-up mix up brightened the bulletin of the First Presbyterian Church of Phoenix: "Remember in prayer Mrs. Walter ...., Mr. Clarence ...., the high school every Tuesday at 6:30 except as announced otherwise."

✠

The following Christmas, the same church bulletin gave exciting ecclesiastical authority to, "Sing, choirs of angels, sin in exultation." The pastor was hard put to shift the blame.

✠

A strip tease artist at the carnival upset the town, so the good people called in the ministers of the Baptist, Presbyterian and Methodist churches to serve as an investigating committee. The next day the local newspaper headlined their report: THREE PASTORS WEIGH HER FAN DANCE; FIND IT WANTON.

7.
Reverent Repartee

America still has more marriages than divorces, proving that preachers can still outtalk lawyers.

✝

"Drinking," warned a pastor, addressing his church Men's Club, "makes such fools of people, (and most people are such fools to begin with), that it is compounding a felony."

✝

A know-it-all young scientist was at a dinner party, and across from him was the local minister. The scientist had much, too much, to say about Darwin and his "origin of the species," etc. "I can't see that it would make any difference to me," he said loftily, "If my grandfather *was* an ape."

This held everybody in silence for a moment. Then the preacher gently said, "No, I can't see that it would, to you. But it must have made a great difference to your grandmother."

✝

Across the street from the Methodist manse, a wealthy asbestos manufacturer built a mansion. His family then proceeded to "live it up" in very worldly fashion, and there was much partying and drinking. This bothered the good preacher, but he was too kind to say anything about them. One day, however, he did remark to his wife, "They seem to have great faith in their asbestos."

✠

"If he had his conscience removed," said the long-suffering pastor of one layman, "it would be a minor operation."

✠

In another town a minister had worked long and hard on his sermon, and the delivery of it on Sunday morning had started off well. But as he was approaching the conclusion, he became acutely aware that he had lost most of his listeners.

When he finished, he added softly, "I hope it's true."

The congregation was startled by that, and sat up in full attention. "I hope it's true," said the preacher again. "Because if it is true that you can learn while you sleep, I will have the best informed congregation in town."

✠

"I can't git anything out of going to church," one man snapped.

The kindly minister countered that by saying, "We make a living by what we get but we make a life by what we give."

✠

A preacher got up and said, "Next Sunday I will preach about liars. In preparation, I want you to read the seventeenth chapter of St. Mark."

The next Sunday he opened by asking how many

had read that seventeenth chapter. More than a dozen dutiful hands went up.

"Um hummm, thank you," said the minister. "Now I can truly preach about liars. St. Mark has only sixteen chapters."

✠

"Ho, ho," said the good humored vicar in London, "I can make a pun on any subject. Just try me. Will someone name a subject?"

A parishioner called out, "The Queen!"

Quick as a wink the vicar punned, "The Queen is not a subject!"

✠

In Montgomery, Alabama, four cows leaped out of a passing truck and fled through traffic right into the First Presbyterian Church. Some excitement ensued, but no damage.

"It just shows you," cracked the alert Rev. Merle C. Patterson, "that we have a church with an open door."

✠

Over in Rusk County, Texas, a pastor was walking along a country road, and stopped to chat with a farmer who was running a mowing machine over a field. "And what does your son do, Hiram?" he asked the man.

"He's a boot black up there in Dallas."

"Ah, I see," the witty pastor exclaimed. "So you make hay while the son shines!"

✠

The Rev. Sam Lindamood met one of his flock on the street and saw that the man was tipsy. "Larry, my friend," he cried, "haven't I told you often from my pulpit that whiskey is your enemy?"

"I know you have, parson. And you also told us we are to love our enemies." With which the man beamed triumphantly.

Parson Sam got in the last word, "Yes, but I did not tell you to swallow them!"

✠

"All rumors should be fitted with girdles," the minister told the gossipy women's club of his church.

"Why?" they demanded.

"To keep them from spreading."

✠

At the great religio-psychiatric clinic of a famous church in New York City, a patient stayed with the counselor for hours. When he departed, the pastor asked, "What was wrong with that poor man?"

"He said he had a split personality," replied the counselor.

"And what did you tell him to do?"

"Well," the weary psychiatrist allegedly sighed, "I finally told him to go chase himself."

✠

The date was April 10. The nation was in turmoil as usual, and poor Sam Dithers told his pastor he was going crazy trying to fill out Form 1040.

"Stop trying," the good minister advised, "and hire an expert accountant. Remember, we are living in the only country in the world where it takes more intelligence to make out the income tax return than it does to make the income."

Fred Fell tells of the preacher who borrowed $1,000 every Friday afternoon and returned it to the bank every Monday morning. Finally the banker asked how come. "What do you do with it, parson?"

"Nothing," admitted the good man. "But mine is a fashionable church in the Country Club district. And with $1,000 in my pocket every Sunday morning, I can get up there in front of those people and preach!"

✠

"A cold," says my preacher friend Carl Soults, waving his handkerchief, "is both positive and negative. Sometimes the eyes have it, sometimes the nose."

✠

The congregation went into a field for the annual church picnic. About dessert time the choir leader said, "This certainly is an ideal place for a picnic."

"It evidently is," agreed the minister. "Fifty thousand ants can't be wrong."

✠

Mrs. Parishioner came in indignation to confer with her pastor because her modern minded son in college had grown a full beard. She felt that maybe the minister could talk the boy into "getting back to decency and looking normal again."

The pastor was smarter than she. "Madam," said he, "I have to tell you that most of the men who have had greatest influence on my life and whom I most admire, wore beards — Moses, Jesus, my grandfather, Uncle Sam, Santa Claus. Let your son keep his. I may grow one myself."

"Too many of us wait to pray until we are in trouble," the pastor warned. "I suggest tht some morning you wake up and say, 'Anything I can do for YOU today, Lord?'"

✠

"It is not always sinful to make a mistake," the pastor told us at Men's Club. "But it can be very sinful if you give an encore."

✠

"Stop knocking our American democracy," the Rev. Dr. Billy Boice thundered at us in Kiwanis Club meeting. "It is true that in our nation the votes of the stupid ones, the evil ones, the vicious and greedy ones, all count. But under any other system of government, those are the kind of people who would be running the whole show."

✠

"Hardening of the heart," the Rev. George Hall told his people, "is infinitely more dangerous than hardening of the arteries."

✠

The Rev. Dr. Heightone had gone to another town, the Rev. Dr. Grandnaime couldn't report for the local pulpit until some time in the Fall.
"And so," the church session gravely instructed good Rev. Joe Interim, "do not set up any policies that may have to be changed later."
Joe Interim glared at his employers and said, "Gen-

tlemen, I am not here selling insurance. I am selling salvation, and the policies for all of us were set up approximately 2,000 years ago."

✝

Sebe Cornstalk was slyly trying to pull his pastor's leg. "Parson, I worry about a mighty big problem. I just can't figure how I am going to pull my undershirt on over my wings Up There."

The parson came right back at him. "That's not it, Sebe. *Your* problem is how you are going to get your hat on over your horns."

✝

Paddy O'Brien was in jail again, and the kindly priest called on him there. "Yis, your riv-rince, sor," Paddy was truly contrite — head low — "in a moment of weakness I stole a grand piano."

"A grand piano, was it!" the priest was shocked. "Paddy, whatever would you have done in a moment of strength?"

✝

For half an hour the good pastor had listened patiently to his men's group sounding off about the dangers of life today. Finally he spoke out: "Gentlemen, if you think *you* live a hazardous existence, consider the long tailed cat in a house full of rocking chairs."

✝

When the program ran short at our church men's meeting one night, the pastor stood up, smiled and announced, "The chairman has asked me to come before you and say something funny."

Deacon Loren Pedrick, quick trigger member of the minister's golf foursome, called out, "You'll tell us when you say it, won't you?"

The pastor nodded benevolently and replied, "I'll tell *you*, Loren. The others will know."

✝

The Rev. Bill Vogel called in his friend K. E. Mackey, a Certified Public Accountant, to help straighten out his family finances.

"Bill, how do you budget your salary?" the CPA asked.

"Well, I have to allow ten per cent for the church. Then I budget 35 per cent for clothing for mama and the children and me, thirty per cent for amusement and incidentals, and forty per cent for food and doctor bills."

"But that adds up to 115 per cent."

"Heavens," exclaimed Pastor Bill, "don't I know it!"

✝

"The sum total of our national debt is some total!" warned the pastor at his Men's Club.

✝

Our big church sanctuary was refrigerated last summer for the first time, and while the cost was high, requiring much sacrifice, we are all delighted with the results. "I could build a sermon on that," threatens the pastor. "We also face cost and sacrifice if we are to escape some other heat that I frequently mention."

The preacher was making his hospital calls. As he stopped beside the bed of one of his more sinful laymen, the man awoke and spoke. "Why are the blinds drawn, pastor?"

"To tell you the truth, Jim, there is a big fire across the street, and I didn't want you to wake up and think that your operation had been a failure."

✠

Poor impecunious Dr. Thredbaire of Doldrum Seminary was awakened at 2 a.m. by a burglar in his bedroom. The burglar drew a pistol and snarled, "Don't move or I'll kill you. I am only hunting for your money."

Replied Dr. Thredbaire, "Well just let me get up and light a candle. Then I can help you hunt."

✠

Dr. Saddlie Thredbaire was often hungry on his minuscule salary. One day a parishioner brought him a string of fine brook trout, but in presenting them said hesitantly, "Sir, I guess I ought to tell you that these trout were caught on Sunday."

Dr. Thredbaire gazed hungrily at them and declared, "Well, the trout aren't to blame for that. Thank you very much for them."

✠

A college was honoring a group of ministers, and had them on the graduation platform awarding honorary degrees. Out front, an enthusiastic student shouted, "Long live our preachers!"

From his chair on the rostrum, Dr. Saddlie Thredbaire answered, "On what?"

One of good Dr. Charles Ehrhardt's goofy parishioners came into his study one day and said, "Oh, Reverend, whatever am I to do? The ghosts of my departed kinfolk come and perch on the tops of the fence posts around my house. They just sit there, staring. I am frightened badly. Whatever shall I do?"

Kindly Dr. Ehrhardt thought for a moment, then offered a sensible and helpful suggestion — "Sharpen the posts!"

✠

The preacher was dangerously ill, couldn't have visitors. But when one neighbor, an agnostic, called to pay his respects, the preacher asked that he be sent in anyway.

"I sure appreciate this," said the agnostic. "But how is it you asked to see me, when you deny admission to your close friends?"

"That's easy to explain," said the dying preacher. "I am very confident of seeing my close friends in heaven. But this is probably the last chance I'll have to see you."

✠

The very elderly minister of a very impoverished church was dying, and the deacons had gathered at his bedside.

"Oh pastor," one cried dismally, "we appreciate all you have done for us, and we shall give you the grandest funeral ever. We will hire ten buses and take the whole congregation to the services."

"We can't afford any such costly outlay," snapped a second Deacon. "We will simply hire two limousines to haul your family and the church staff."

"That's also a sinful outlay which we can't afford," put in still another. "We'll get along with only the hearse and one car, and borrow the car from the storekeeper."

Whereupon the dying pastor lifted his head slightly and said, "Just hand me my pants, gentlemen, and I'll walk to the cemetery."

✠

One minister's congregation kept going fishing on Sunday mornings. Since fish were biting exceedingly well that spring, it seemed that practically all the members were tempted. So one Sunday at 4 a.m. the good preacher got up and joined his flock at the boat pier, went out with them, corralled all of them into a protected area, and held services on the water. Next Sunday morning his church was full.

✠

Two preachers were avid fishermen — never on Sunday, of course. One Monday at 6 p.m. George Hall came upon his colleague Elmer Ray, after a long afternoon of it. "Greetings, George," said Elmer. "There sure are plenty of fish in this lake."

"Yes," nodded George sadly, stowing his tackle. "And I'm the one who left them there."

✠

The depressed gent was in his pastor's study pouring out his woes. The pastor counseled him to count his blessings and be thankful.

"Thankful!" he growled. "What have I to be thankful for? Why, I can't pay a single one of my many debts."

"Well, then," said the preacher gently, "be thankful that you are not one of your creditors."

✠

"It's easy enough to pick out the best people," declared the Rev. Tom Barker at church Men's Club. "In fact, they'll help you do it."

✠

A fatuous tourist accosted gentle Dr. Dallas Turner one day in the resort town of Laguna Beach, California, and asked, "Say, preacher, have any big men ever been born in this little town?"

Dr. Turner, though the last man on earth to hurt anybody's feelings, couldn't resist saying, "I am afraid not, sir. The best we ever produce are babies."

✠

A very mediocre author was in the membership of a Presbyterian Church, and he had written a number of poor biographies. One day he approached the distinguished pastor there and rather pompously said, "For years I have been wanting to do a book about you, pastor. When you die, I hope to write your biography."

"Yes, I know," the preacher nodded. "That's one of the things that keeps me going."

8.
Wedding Daze

"The best man at a wedding," grumbled the best man at the wedding, "never has a chance to prove it."

✠

The Rev. Dr. Thredbaire, back home, was telling his wife about the wedding he had performed. "I am afraid, though, that his married life will not be particularly happy."

"Why not, dear?"

"Well, I was watching the bride's family all through the ceremony. They looked far too cheerful to suit me."

✠

There's really no need for the father of the bride to be jittery at the wedding. He is completely inconsequential. All he has to do is to walk down the aisle with her, wait until the preacher ritualistically asks "Who giveth this woman away?" then reply "I do" or, "Her mother and I do." So — at a Montana wedding the preacher explained all that and told papa he needn't rehearse.

So guess what happened. Nervous papa stood down there shakily, heard the question, and said loud enough for all the church to hear, "Her mother and her father and I do!"

In one city the minister had just finished marrying a beautiful young thing to a plumber. After the ceremony the plumber edged up close to the minister and whispered, "I ain't got any money to pay you, but I'll come out to your house and fix your gas meter so it won't register."

✛

It was two months after the wedding, and old friends kept joshing the father of the bride, asking if he had recovered from the strain. "Oh, I'm just about emotionally normal again," he confesed. "But financial normalcy will require at least another five years."

✛

A young minister married a young soprano from his choir and they started on their honeymoon by train. He gave the Pullman porter two dollars not to tell anybody they were bride and groom. But next morning at breakfast, everybody stared at them, and this worried the preacher. He called the porter aside and asked, "Did you tell anybody on the train that we were just married?"

"No suh, I didn't tell a soul," the porter said. "I told everybody that you-all was single."

✛

"Aha, my boy," said an uncle to his nephew, "I congratulate you. I hear you are engaged to one of the beautiful Smith twins."

"Yes, sir. Thank you sir."

"But," the uncle looked puzzled, "how do you ever manage to tell those identical twins apart?"

The boy gave a satisfied shrug of his shoulders and replied, "I don't try."

A pastor, counseling a couple having marital troubles asked, "You say that your husband beats you constantly?"

"No, sir," admitted the young bride. "When the weather is nice he goes to the race track."

✠

The college-age girl, none too bright, went to her pastor for counsel about a certain young man.

"Before you get serious about him," the good pastor advised, "be very sure that he is always kind."

"Oh, I *am* sure. Why, only last Tuesday he told me that he put his shirt on a horse that was scratched."

✠

Two pastors were discussing their effectiveness as marrying preachers. Said one, "I can think of one couple I married, and the man has spent every evening at home for 25 years."

"Remarkable!" his colleague nodded. "That's what I call true love."

"No. The doctor calls it paralysis."

✠

His bride was crying when George returned home from work. "Your mother has insulted me," she lamented.

"My mother? How? She is a thousand miles from here."

"A letter came to you this morning. It was in your mother's handwriting, so naturally I opened it."

He nodded, but with scant enthusiasm.

"Every word was written to you, George. Except for the postscript. That's where she insulted me."

"In the postscript? What did she say there?"

"She said: 'P.S. — Dear Maisie, don't forget to give this letter to my George. I want him to read it, too.'"

✠

The good Rev. Dallas Turner performed the ceremony, blessed the young couple, and turned to the young man. "So, my friend, you have come to the end of all your troubles," he beamed.

Months passed. Then one day the groom happened onto Dr. Turner again — "Sir, I thought you told me at the wedding that I had come to the end of all my troubles. Did I hear you correctly?"

"Yes, surely, son. But perhaps I neglected to say which end."

✠

The pastor was on duty one afternoon as marriage counselor, listening quietly while Mrs. McWorry talked about her husband. Presently she said, "And Reverend, every time he traps me into discussing something calmly, sensibly, like mature adults, I lose!"

✠

Again, the same pastoral counselor asked another party: "Why, Mrs. Smith, did you hit your husband with a chair?"

"Because I couldn't lift the piano," she answered.

The kindly old preacher encountered a woman at whose wedding he had officiated. "And does your husband always live up to the promises made during his courtship days?" he asked.

"He sure does," she snapped. "In those days he kept saying he wasn't good enough for me, and he has been proving it ever since."

✛

Dr. Dallas Turner of Laguna Beach, California, married his pretty daughter to a handsome young man. He naturally was emotionally involved too, and so he forgot some of the ritual. At the end he had to run down the aisle, out the front door of the church, and catch the happy couple getting into their car to go honeymooning. There he solemnly said, "I now pronounce you man and wife!"

✛

It seems that King Solomon's 999th wife was feeling coy one afternoon. So, flirting a little, she tickled his nose with an ostrich feather and said, "Sol, tell me — do you really love me? Am I important to you?"

Solomon — a man of wisdom, remember — replied: "Darling, you are one in a thousand!"

✛

Dr. Charles Kendall, beloved minister in Hollywood, was interviewing two candidates for marriage, and naturally he wanted to be sure that everything was on the up and up. He asked gently, "Were either of you ever married before?"

Snapped the woman, "Before what?"

Brides are supposed to be shrewd. But we males aren't completely without shrewdness, either. At age forty, a confirmed bachelor finally married the village shrew, a female known for her quarrelsome disposition and temper. Of course his friends asked him why he ever wanted to marry such a woman.

"I married her as a penance," said he, humbly. "I have enjoyed too good a time as a bachelor, and I am afraid I might never get to heaven unless I suffer some here on earth."

Of course, gossips carried that news to his bride, as he knew they would. She flew into a rage, raved for hours, and declared that she would not let that man get the best of her.

So to punish him, she forced herself to be sweet, kind, and considerate, a model wife for the remainder of her days.

✝

One handsome young bachelor preacher, Clyde James, new in his parish, suddenly fell in love with the sassy looking soprano who had just joined the choir. After only three dates, he fell to his knees one night, and not for prayer, either.

"Gloria," he soared to the stars in his impassioned burst of romance, "I know I am not much. A preacher will always be called to a life of service. I do not have a fine limousine and chauffeur like Edgar Meyer has; I'll never have a mansion and a yacht like Ed Meyer, but I *do* love you, Gloria. Will you be mine?"

"You're right nice, Clyde. But tell me — where is this Meyer person?"

"Yes," admitted the pastor to his men's class, "men may be more intelligent than women. But you never see a woman marrying a dumb man because of his shape."

✠

There was a man who was engaged to one of the McDougall twins, and a friend said he couldn't see how the prospective bridegroom told them apart.

"Easy," avowed the young swain. "Martha always blushes when we meet."

✠

Much of what America calls religion stems at least theoretically from the Pilgrim Fathers. So — the big Congregational Church hired a "name" speaker to come and address its annual congregational meeting. He did so, and chose to praise the Pilgrim Fathers at length.

At the end, a firm-lipped lady stood up to ask a question: "Sir, what about the Pilgrim mothers?"

Taken slightly aback, the orator could only ask, "Well, what about them?"

Exclaimed the lady, "What about them indeed! They endured every hardship that the Pilgrim Fathers endured, and in addition, they endured the Pilgrim Fathers themselves!"

✠

"Now I know why Solomon took 13 years to build his house," growled the muchly married young man to his pastor.

"Why, son?"

"He had 1000 wives making suggestions."

A wedding ceremony was under way. The bride had been married before, so Grandmother brought the bride's three lively children to the church. But they squirmed, they talked, they giggled, until Gram had to get firm with them.

"If you kids don't stop that and be quiet," she warned in a loud murmur, "I won't bring you next time!"

✛

A grim-faced young man stormed into his minister's office and said, "I just came to ask you if you consider it right for any person to profit by the mistake of others."

"Certainly not," said the preacher.

"Well then, I want you to return that ten dollars I gave you last June for marrying me."

✛

The young male hippie — long hair, beads, dirt, sandals, guitar and all — went to the license bureau for a marriage license.

At the proper place the clerk asked, "Is the bride-to-be a Protestant or Catholic?"

The young man paused, frowned, and said, "No, not exactly."

That stymied the clerk for a moment. But, trying to be tactful, he said, "Well, under 'religion' I'll just put down 'None.'"

"Oh, no, sir," the hippie spoke quickly now. "I *know* she was never one of those!"

9.
Younger Generations

The preacher was making an important point in his sermonette to a group of boys. "Remember always," said he, "that it is more blessed to give than to receive. Do you all agree with that?"

"I sure do," piped up Butch Dugan. "My Dad uses that motto in his business all the time."

The pastor beamed. "Ah! Isn't that fine! Indeed yes. And what is your father's business, my little man?"

Replied Butch: "He's a prize-fighter."

✙

One woman who was interested in spiritualism was always going to seances, "readings," etc. One day she took her little boy along, so that the medium might help him talk to his dear departed father.

Things went pretty well, too. After the medium turned the lights low and mumbled some things low sure enough papa's remembered voice came into the room.

"Hey there, Pop!" exclaimed Johnny. "Where are you?"

The male voice intoned, "I am in heaven, my boy."

"How about that!" Johnny was interested. "And are you an angel, Pop?"

"Oh, yes, my boy."

"An angel with harps and wings?"

"That is correct."

Johnny paused to consider that, then continued

73

eagerly, "Say Pop, tell me — what do you measure from tip to tip?"

✠

Up in Fond du Lac, Wisconsin, Norman S. Jennings told his Sunday-school class that they are here to help others. Inevitably, of course, one bright lad asked, "Well, what are the others here for?"

✠

Navy Commander Jerry F. Detwiler, a distinguished Presbyterian church leader, has a little daughter named Sharie. One Sabbath noon he asked her what she had learned in Sunday school that day.

Replied Sharie: "We learned about the ten commanders. They are always broke."

✠

Ten-year-old Merton Hill, while a faithful Sunday school attender, nevertheless wasn't *about* to let himself be brainwashed. On this Sabbath the class teacher was pouring it on, emphasizing the great sin of murder and the great compassion that God has for all sinners. He tried gently to say that maybe capital punishment wasn't the best thing for a local man who had just murdered somebody; perhaps life imprisonment would suffice. Feeling that he had made his moral point, the teacher asked young Mert, "Now what punishment should that man have?"

"Hang him!" growled young Merton instantly.

The teacher swallowed hard and plunged in again. He rehashed the moral point; talked about tolerance, forgiveness, compassion, the great concepts of the

Christian teaching, the questionable value of execution as a deterrent for crime in any event. From Mert's rapt interest, the man felt that now for sure he had gotten through to the boy. So he asked again, "Now what punishment should that murderer have, Merton?"

Growled young Mert, "Shoot him!"

✠

The minister had one of those modern teen-age sons — the kind that objects to everything and carries signs around to prove it. Of course, such a young sophisticate couldn't think of attending the church picnic. It wasn't held, anyway. When the minister came home, he reported that only half a dozen people had showed up for the picnic because of hail and rain.

"Good grief," exclaimed the boy, "if there is anything I simply can't stand, it's a fair-weather fanatic!"

✠

Because of his naughtiness, his mother felt it necessary to reprimand four-year-old Larry Detwiler and sent him to be alone in his room for an hour. But after half an hour, soft-hearted mother poked her head in the door.

"All right," Larry spoke threateningly, "I've been talking to God about you."

✠

At the Valley Presbyterian Church in Scottsdale, Arizona, several years ago, the preacher learned that Mrs. Mamie Eisenhower, wife of the great general and president, was coming there to worship. Of course the preacher was in something of a dither, but he lined up the sweet little Sunday-school children to welcome her.

All the kids lined up on the lawn — except one individualist, a six-year-old boy. "Why don't you come with the others, Roscoe?" the minister asked.

"Because," said the lad, realistically, "*My* daddy is a Democrat!"

✠

"Myrrh," a little girl defined when her Sunday-school teacher asked, "is what our mother cat gives to her kittens when she licks them."

✠

The Rev. Mr. Shortfunds had been preaching hard to his congregation, when he got a call to another church at more than double his current salary. He felt duty bound to pray over it, to see if he should go. Next day somebody asked his little son if he had decided to take the offer.

"I can't say for sure," the lad replied, "because papa is still praying. But mama is packing."

✠

Mother was teaching young Chuck to say his prayers. "You mean," he questioned, "if I pray, I'll get everything I want?"

She hedged a little, of course. "Everything that's good for you, sweetheart."

Chuck shrugged. "Then why should I bother? I get that anyway."

At a church in Kentucky on Palm Sunday, the junior choir sang three beautiful numbers, then sat down to hear the sermon. But young Butch Hawkins stood back up and walked out.

Unperturbed, the preacher suggested to his flock: "Doubtless Butch is accustomed to leaving the room during commercials."

✝

But there is a record of one juvenile prayer that every adult would approve. It was bedtime, and sweet little Jennifer was kneeling, and her Mommy suggested, "Be sure to include Grandmother in your prayers, dear. Ask God to let her be happy and live to be very old."

"No," said Jennifer, after a moment of reflection. "I love Grandmother, she is full of fun. I'd rather pray that God lets her stay young."

✝

Then there is that legendary lad who, bored by long, pious Wednesday night sessions in church, finally got to see a circus then reported to his grandmother, "Grannie, if you'd ever go to a circus just once, you'd never want to attend prayer meeting again."

✝

One lovely young lady has registered a perfectly logical complaint with us ushers: "Please do not again seat my parents in the pew just behind me and my boyfriend."

Then there was the doting father who observed four-year-old Sonny busy with his blocks. "What are you building, son?" Dad asked.

"A church," the lad replied. "Sh-h-h, we must be very quiet."

Fine! Now there was unexpected reverence, to be encouraged. "Why are we to be quiet in church, son?"

"Because," said the bright boy, "the people are all asleep."

✠

I once was showing the same lad the extravagantly lush and beautiful flowers in our sun-kissed yard in Phoenix, Arizona, one February. I told him such winter flowers were a gift of God, and that the snowbound East couldn't enjoy such bounty in winter. "Why?" he demanded, "Isn't there any God back East?"

✠

At a church in the state of New York a little boy escaped from Sunday school and climbed 99 feet to the tip top of the steep church steeple. He didn't say anything when he left, and wasn't missed, and doubtless was having himself a high time, until the big bell right near him let out a thunderous *BONG.* . . . *BONG!* That scared the living daylights out of him, so he set up a howl that must have been heard in heaven itself. He was stuck up there and couldn't get down.

Of course a crowd gathered, and of course his brave father climbed to rescue him. All the way, father

78

looked up, encouraging his son to be strong, to hold tight. But when he got to the top and looked down, *he* got scared and couldn't return!

While everybody else rushed around with ladders, ropes and advice, the boy's mother calmly climbed the stairway inside the steeple, opened a little service door near the top, and pulled her menfolks safely inside.

✠

Allegedly, the scientists in Russia had perfected an atomic machine that would completely control the weather, the professor told his class of budding young scientists. He added that they had made public demonstration of it on February 1 when a great sleet and snow storm was predicted.

"Did it work?" the class asked eagerly.

"Well, no," the prof reluctantly admitted. "The machine was out of adjustment, and Moscow suffered the worst blizzard in its history."

One young Christian in the class then shouted, "Well, hurray for God!"

✠

"Not only are children a great comfort in old age," declared the Rev. Bill Vogel, "but they help you get there sooner."

✠

"You will have a happier life," the pastor warned his pretty sixteen-year-old daughter, "if you avoid trying to convert a boy friend into a buy friend."

"If I read my fifteen-year-old daughter's mental processes correctly," groused one pastor, "our world during the millennium will be inhabited only by herself, a few carefully chosen girl friends, and an endless multitude of sixteen-year-old boys with driver's licenses and red convertibles."

✠

The atheist wrote: GOD IS NOWHERE. Fortunately, his little daughter rewrote it: GOD IS NOW HERE, and thus got the matter straightened out.

✠

Little Buttercup Butterfield, is a three-year-old whose mother overheard this bedtime prayer: "Thank you, Mister God, for the Happy Birfday party. Let's have another one soon, hunh, shall we, hunh?"

✠

At Phoenix, Arizona, the fine baseball team at Grand Canyon College, a Southern Baptist institution, had won 19 straight games and lost none, with the main part of the season just beginning.

So little Biffy Buff, aged six, was overheard at bedtime prayer: "Please dear God, keep Pop from making a fool of himself rooting so hard for the Grand Canyon team this year."

✠

Definition of "conscience." "That's what hurts," declared a small boy, "when everything else feels so good."